Staffing to Support
Business Strategy

Staffing to Support
Business Strategy

Jean M. Phillips and Stanley M. Gully

Staffing Strategically Series

Society for Human Resource Management | Alexandria, Virginia | USA
www.shrm.org | © 2009

This publication is designed to provide accurate and authoritative information regarding the subject matter covered. It is sold with the understanding that neither the publisher nor the author is engaged in rendering legal or other professional service. If legal advice or other expert assistance is required, the services of a competent, licensed professional should be sought. The federal and state laws discussed in this book are subject to frequent revision and interpretation by amendments or judicial revisions that may significantly affect employer or employee rights and obligations. Readers are encouraged to seek legal counsel regarding specific policies and practices in their organizations.

This book is published by the Society for Human Resource Management (SHRM®). The interpretations, conclusions, and recommendations in this book are those of the authors and do not necessarily represent those of the publishers.

Copyright © 2009 Phillips, Gully, and Associates. All rights reserved.

This publication may not be reproduced, stored in a retrieval system, or transmitted in whole or in part, in any form or by any means, electronic, mechanical, photocopying, recording, or otherwise, without the prior written permission of the Society for Human Resource Management, 1800 Duke Street, Alexandria, VA 22314.

The Society for Human Resource Management (SHRM) is the world's largest association devoted to human resource management. Representing more than 250,000 members in over 140 countries, the Society serves the needs of HR professionals and advances the interests of the HR profession. Founded in 1948, SHRM has more than 575 affiliated chapters within the United States and subsidiary offices in China and India. Visit SHRM Online at www.shrm.org.

Library of Congress Cataloging-in-Publication Data

Phillips, Jean, 1969-
  Staffing to support business strategy / Jean M. Phillips, Stanley M. Gully.
    p. cm. — (Staffing strategically series)
  Includes bibliographical references and index.
  ISBN 978-1-58644-161-6
  1. Employee selection. 2. Personnel management. 3. Strategic planning. I. Gully, Stanley Morris. II. Title.
  HF5549.5.S38P492 2009
  658.3'01—dc22
                              2009037429

Staffing Strategically Series

ASSESSING EXTERNAL JOB CANDIDATES

ASSESSING INTERNAL JOB CANDIDATES

THE LEGAL CONTEXT OF STAFFING

STAFFING FORECASTING AND PLANNING

STAFFING TO SUPPORT BUSINESS STRATEGY

Contents

Introduction 1

Resource-Based View of the Firm 3

Business Strategy 9

Talent Philosophy 19

Deriving Staffing Strategy 27

Strategic Staffing Decisions 31

Competitive Talent Advantage 47

Goals of Strategic Staffing 51

Summary 57

Endnotes 59

Index 63

Acknowledgments 67

About the Authors 69

Additional SHRM-Published Books 71

Introduction

Why does one company succeed and another company fail? Most people believe a company must focus on its strategic, financial, and technological capabilities to compete successfully. We now know that these important capabilities must be supplemented with organizational capabilities generated by attracting, retaining, motivating, and developing talented employees.[1] Staffing therefore plays a central role in creating and enhancing any organization's competitive advantage. As Steve Ballmer, CEO of Microsoft, said,

"You may have a technology or a product that gives you an edge, but your people determine whether you develop the next winning technology or product."[2]

Organizations that pursue different competitive strategies require different staffing strategies to execute them. Procter & Gamble (P&G) must continually introduce new and improved products such as multi-blade razors and tooth-whitening toothpaste to stay competitive. Companies such as P&G need to foster creativity and risk-taking among certain employees. On the other hand, companies such as Lexus, which focus on delivering the best quality or value to customers, need to stress operations and improving work processes to reduce costs and improve product quality. These companies are more likely to need team players who are trainable and able to follow standardized procedures.

Acquiring, developing, and retaining the right talent helps to create the organizational capability and intellectual capital that drives business strategy execution. This potential is well known by companies such as Time, Inc., the world's largest magazine publisher, with products such as *People, Sports Illustrated,* and *Fortune* that reach total audiences of more than 300 million readers. Kerry Bessey, Time's senior vice president of Human Resources, states, "HR's mission is building capability for Time's business .... Our executives view us as management partners because we recognize this business is about talent—it's what drives the quality of products that connect to readers."[3]

This book first describes the resource-based view of the firm, then covers the role of business strategy and competitive advantage in determining a firm's staffing needs. We describe what we mean by an organization's talent philosophy and discuss how talent philosophies influence HR strategy and staffing strategy. We also discuss nine strategic staffing decisions all firms must make. After reading this book, you should understand the role of staffing in creating and sustaining a competitive advantage, and in executing different types of business strategies.

Resource-Based View of the Firm

Most organizations recognize that a large budget and state-of-the-art facilities do not guarantee success. Success really depends on employees' motivations, competencies, and skills. The resource-based view of the firm describes how employees' motivations, competencies, and skills can help to create a sustained competitive advantage.

What Is the Resource-Based View of the Firm?

The resource-based view of the firm proposes that a company's resources and competencies can produce a sustained competitive advantage by creating value for customers by lowering costs, providing something of unique value, or some combination of the two.[4] To create value, the hiring programs, policies, and practices of an organization must either lower the costs of the organization's products or services, enhance the differentiation of the organization's products or services in the eyes of customers, or both. To the extent that staffing influences who has the opportunity and desire to pursue an employment relationship with the organization, staffing serves as a gatekeeper in influencing the level and composition of an organization's talent. This can add value to the organization through employees' competency levels, experience, judgment, social relationships, and so on.

Human resources can be a source of competitive advantage because they meet the criteria for being a source of sustainable competitive advantage: they add value to the firm, are rare, cannot be imitated, and cannot easily be substituted with other things. Other companies cannot necessarily replicate another firm's capabilities just by imitating the competitor's HR practices.[5]

The resource-based view of the firm focuses attention on the quality of the skills of a company's workforce at various levels, as well as on the quality of the motivational climate created by management.[6] HR management is valued not only for its role in *implementing a given competitive scenario but also for its role in generating strategic capability*.[7] Staffing has the potential to create organizations that are more intelligent and flexible than their competitors, and that exhibit superior levels of cooperation and performance.[8]

Requirements of a Competitive Advantage

Peoples' efforts, talents, knowledge, and skills matter to organizations. If you don't believe this is true, then fire all of your organization's employees and replace them with cheaper workers. Few successful organizations would accept this challenge because they understand that their people are the key to their performance and survival. A competitive advantage is something that a company can do differently from its competitors that allows it to perform better, survive, and succeed in its industry. Sometimes an organization's competitive advantage is defined by its technology. Other times, innovative product lines, low-cost products, or excellent customer service drive competitive advantage. In every case, the company's employees create, enhance, or implement the company's competitive advantage.

How do people make a difference? At companies such as Microsoft and Google, key technology is devised, implemented, and updated by the people who create and use it. Employees at Apple Computer, Pfizer, and 3M create and sell new and innovative product lines. Employees identify and implement the systematic manufacturing system improvements that create low-cost, high-quality automobiles at Hyundai. Finally, customer service at Starbucks is all about employee-customer interactions and experiences. In every case, employees influence and implement key drivers of business success. From where do these employees come? It all begins with the staffing process.

Jay Barney identifies the five criteria[9] (in Table 1) that a resource must meet to provide an organization with a sustainable competitive advantage.

Table 1. Requirements of a Competitive Advantage

1. It must be valuable to the firm by exploiting opportunities and/or neutralizing threats in an organization's environment.
2. It must be rare among the company's current and future competition.
3. It must not be easily imitated by other firms.
4. It must not be easily substituted or replaced with another resource.
5. The company must be organized to be able to exploit the resource.

Value

Staffing activities can create value for a firm because they can help it to exploit opportunities and/or neutralize threats. The return on staffing investments and the retention and performance of employees can be increased by rigorously evaluating the effectiveness of various staffing practices and targeting staffing activities to identify and attract the best types of applicants for the organization's needs. Providing applicants with realistic information about the job and organization can also help reduce subsequent turnover, reducing overall labor costs and improving productivity.[10] Hiring people who do a better job for the same pay is also a way that staffing investments can create value.

The potential of strategic staffing to create value and a sustainable competitive advantage for an organization has been recognized by investors as well. An Ernst & Young study found that institutional investors are more likely to buy stock based on a company's ability to attract talent, suggesting that the quality of a company's staffing practices can differentiate it to investors.[11] Staffing thus appears to meet the value requirement of creating a competitive advantage.

Rarity

Value creation alone is not enough to produce sustainable competitive advantage. For a company to outperform competitors, its staffing practices must also result in a set of rare workforce attributes. The ability to identify and attract rare talent varies across organizations. For example, some organizations such as Google and Costco are able to hire and retain the best talent at a greater rate than their competitors, distinguishing the competencies of their workforces. Because strategic staffing practices can increase an organization's ability to identify and attract rare talent, staffing meets the rarity requirement for providing a competitive advantage.[12]

Inimitability

If an organization's strategic staffing practices are imitable or easily copied by a competitor, the organization's resulting talent will not be as differentiable from the talent of its competitors. The ability of competitors to copy an organization's staffing practices is determined by: the availability of unique attributes in the labor market; the ambiguity surrounding which staffing practices contribute to the acquisition of the valuable and rare employee characteristics; and the difficulty of replicating practices deeply embedded in social relationships, including recruiting networks and longstanding relationships with talent sources. The organization's unique history and the resulting organizational reputation and culture can also influence competitors' ability to copy an organization's staffing practices.[13] Together, these factors make it unlikely that competitors will easily imitate and implement another organization's constellation of staffing practices.

Imagine if an established company, highly respected for its integrity and community philanthropy, simply passed out business cards at a community function that read, "We're hiring!" and provided an Internet address for further information. This well-known and respected organization is likely to receive a more favorable response to this recruiting initiative than a start-up company with little visibility and no reputation. Two companies that do the same thing may not experience the same response to the same staffing initiative. To the extent that many interrelated factors contribute to the success of an organization's staffing effort, it will be difficult for a competitor to copy all of them exactly. If a competitor can copy or imitate an organization's successful staffing methods, the company's competitive advantage will erode. Staffing thus meets the inimitability requirement for providing a competitive advantage.

Substitutability

A staffing practice should have minimal substitutability, or be difficult for another practice to effectively substitute for it. If a staffing practice is to provide a sustainable competitive advantage, then there can be no good substitute for it.[14] If one company successfully recruits by flying an airplane banner over a popular beach near a university known for its technological capabilities and a competitor can effectively reach the same audience by handing out recruiting brochures at the same beach, then neither company will experience a competitive advantage from recruiting beachgoers. Similarly, if a competitor can find a substitute for the type of talent another organization has acquired, neither organization will realize a competitive advantage.

The nature and talents of the people hired through a particular strategic staffing effort are often not substitutable by technology or other alternatives. If an organization attracts and hires experienced talent with an in-depth understanding of its customers and its industry, it will be difficult for competitors to effectively substitute for these qualities. Technology is also unlikely to sufficiently replace what these talented employees contribute. Because most employee contributions to organizations are not substitutable (e.g., intelligence, judgment, and innovation), staffing meets the competitive advantage criteria of nonsubstitutability as well.[15]

Organization of the Company

For talent to be a source of sustained competitive advantage, a company must be organized to take full advantage of the talent it employs.[16] Inconsistencies in the set of HR activities implemented by organizations (e.g., recruitment, selection, compensation, and training systems used) often cause them to work against each other. For example, if an organization is able to recruit and select the top talent it is pursuing, but offers compensation that is well below the market rate for this talent, then it is unlikely to be able to hire or retain them despite the success of the staffing function in identifying and attracting talented individuals. If an organization successfully hires lower-skilled people with the intention of training them in the necessary job skills but the training program is poor, the organization's ability to fully capitalize on its effective staffing system is constrained. It is thus critical that staffing be integrated with the other HR management functions and with other policies and practices throughout the organization. Staffing provides the input into the other aspects of the HR management system, and the success of the staffing function, as well as the rest of the HR management system, is influenced by its degree of integration and consistency with the other components of the system.[17]

Business Strategy

Business strategy defines how a company will compete in its marketplace.[18] The purpose of a business strategy is to determine how a firm "will deploy its resources within its environment and so satisfy its long-term goals, and how to organize itself to implement that strategy."[19] A company's business strategy states what it intends to offer that will create value for its customers and lead it to be preferred over the competition. Business strategy should reflect what the organization's customers want, what the firm wants, and what the firm can cost-effectively deliver. Business strategies are likely to differ across multiple business units in a diversified corporation. Procter & Gamble, IBM, and General Electric have different strategic approaches to ensure success in their various lines of business. Business strategy addresses product choices and methods of gaining competitive advantage, and it hinges on a company's capabilities, strengths, and weaknesses in relation to market characteristics and the capabilities, strengths, and weaknesses of competitors. For a company to successfully execute its business strategy, its HR management policies and practices must fit with its strategy, its competitive environment, and with the immediate business conditions that it faces.[20]

Successful business strategies are grounded in creating and maintaining a sustainable competitive advantage, which exists any time an organization has an edge over rivals in attracting customers and defending itself against competition. Hiring and retaining the right people are critical to business strategy execution, because it is an organization's *people* who are responsible for gaining and keeping a competitive advantage. Michael Treacy and Fred Wiersma have identified many sources of competitive advantage, including having the best-made or cheapest product, providing the best level of customer service, being more convenient to buy from, having shorter product development times, and having a well-known brand name.[21]

Costco's strong and loyal customer base, access to a broad range of high-quality products for a low price, and committed employees give it a competitive advantage over smaller and lesser-known retailers. Although Costco pays its employees substantially more than its closest competitor, Sam's Club, it has similar financial returns on its labor costs due to lower turnover and higher levels of employee productivity.[22] This, in turn, results in a better-qualified workforce and a higher-quality customer experience. According to Michael Porter, to have a competitive advantage a company must ultimately be able to give customers *superior value for their money (a combination of quality, service, and acceptable price)—a better product that is worth a premium price or a good product at a lower price can both be a source of competitive advantage.*[23] Table 2 lists some possible sources of competitive advantage.

Table 2 Sources of Competitive Advantage

Innovation: Develop new products, services, and markets, and improve current ones.
Cost: Be the lowest-cost provider.
Service: Provide the best customer support before, during or after the sale.
Quality: Provide the highest-quality product or service.
Branding: Develop the most positive image.
Distribution: Dominate distribution channels to block competition.
Speed: Excel at getting your product or service to consumers quickly.
Convenience: Be the easiest for customers to do business with.
First to market: Introduce products and services before competitors.

We next discuss business strategy in more detail, as well as how staffing can reinforce the organization's overall business strategy and support its execution.

Types of Business Strategies

A company may create value based on price, technological leadership, customer service, or some combination of these and other factors. Business strategy involves the issue of how to compete, but also encompasses:

- The strategies of different functional areas in the firm;

- How changing industry conditions such as deregulation, product market maturity, and changing customer demographics will be addressed; and
- How the firm as a whole will address the range of strategic issues and choices it faces.

Business strategies are partially planned and partially reactive to changing circumstances. A large number of possible strategies exist for any organization, and an organization may pursue different strategies in different business units. Companies may also pursue more than one strategy at a particular time. According to Michael Porter, businesses can compete successfully by being the cheapest producer, by making unique products valued by consumers, or by applying their expertise in a narrow market segment to meet that segment's particular product or service needs.[24] These three primary business strategies are cost leadership, differentiation, and specialization. Another strategic choice is whether to grow the business, and, if so, how to do it. We next discuss each of these strategies and their implications for what is required of the staffing function.

Cost-Leadership Strategy

Firms pursuing a cost-leadership strategy strive to be the lowest cost producer in an industry for a particular level of product quality. These businesses are typically good at designing products that can be manufactured efficiently (for example, designing products with a minimum number of parts needing assembly) and engineering efficient manufacturing processes to keep production costs and customer prices low. Wal-Mart is a good example of a firm pursuing a cost-leadership strategy.

Organizations pursuing a strategy of keeping costs and prices low try to develop a competitive advantage in operational excellence. Employees in these firms need to identify and follow efficient processes and engage in continuous improvement. Manufacturing and transportation companies frequently adopt this approach. These organizations' operational systems continually look for ways to reduce costs and lower prices while offering a desirable product that competes successfully with competitors' products. Dell Computers, Federal Express, and Wal-Mart are good examples of companies whose competitive advantage is based on operational excellence.

Because most operationally excellent firms require trainable and flexible employees who are able to focus on shorter-term production objectives, who avoid waste, and who are concerned about production costs, employees who display pretentious behavior are not desirable.[25] Because operationally excellent organizations operate with tight margins and rely more on teamwork than individual performance, it is not as helpful to pay the high price required to attract top talent because the return on this investment is not high enough and the resulting pay disparity can hinder effective teamwork. Staffing goals for such an organization's core production workforce include hiring people who are adaptable, efficiency-oriented, trainable, and willing to follow standardized procedures.

Differentiation Strategy

A differentiation strategy calls for the development of a product or service that has unique characteristics valued by customers. The value added by the product's uniqueness may enable the business to charge a premium price for it. The dimensions along which a firm can differentiate include image (Rolex), product durability (Carter's children's clothing), quality (Lexus), safety (Mercedes), and usability (Apple Computer). Some companies, such as Southwest Airlines and ING Direct bank, differentiate themselves from their competitors by pursuing a strategy based on only providing no-frills, basic products and services at a low cost. As we mentioned earlier, companies can pursue more than one strategy at a time. In this case, Southwest Airlines and ING Direct are both cost leaders and differentiators.

Organizations pursuing a differentiation strategy often try to develop a competitive advantage based on product innovation. This requires employees to continually develop new products and services to create its advantage in the market. These companies create and maintain an environment that encourages employees to bring new ideas into the company. These companies then listen to and consider these ideas, however unconventional they might be. For these companies, the frequent introduction of new products is key to staying competitive. This strategy is common in technology and pharmaceutical companies. Johnson & Johnson, Nike, and 3M are good examples of organizations whose competitive advantage is based on product innovation.

Product innovators must protect their entrepreneurial environment. To that end, they recruit, hire, and train employees to fit their innovative culture. That means that instead of selecting job candidates based only on their related experience, they also assess whether a candidate can work cooperatively in teams and whether he or she is open-minded and creative.[26] An organization with a competitive advantage in product innovation would likely seek a core workforce of research and development employees who have an entrepreneurial mind-set, longer-term focus, high tolerance for ambiguity, and an interest in learning and discovery. Employees who need stability and predictability would not fit as well. Individuals able to sift through large amounts of information to identify ideas that lead to new products or services would also be valuable to innovative companies. Firms pursuing a differentiation strategy based on innovation would likely make greater investments in their human resources and focus on hiring highly skilled workers for key research positions.[27]

Because being first to market with the best new products is usually the highest priority of product innovators, cost is less of a barrier when acquiring top talent for key research and development positions. Individual contributions are important for this type of organization, and new hires who understand that pay disparities will exist depending on employees' backgrounds and contributions to new product development and who are motivated by a pay-for-performance system are likely to be good fits. Innovative organizations relying on new product development and organizational flexibility require employees with a wider range of aptitudes and abilities than do organizations in narrow, relatively stable markets relying on a low-cost strategy.[28]

Specialization Strategy

Businesses pursuing a specialization strategy focus on a narrow market segment or niche—a single product, a particular end use, or buyers with special needs—and pursue either a differentiation or cost-leadership strategy within that market segment. Successful businesses following a specialist strategy know their market segment very well, and often enjoy a high degree of customer loyalty. This strategy can be successful if it results in either lower costs than competitors serving the same niche or an ability to offer customers something other competitors do not (e.g., manufacturing nonstandard parts). Red Lobster and Starbucks are examples of companies pursuing a specialization strategy, and Seiko sells a variety of relatively inexpensive but innovative specialty watches with features including compasses and altimeters.

Organizations pursuing a specialization strategy often try to develop a competitive advantage based on customer intimacy and try to deliver unique and customizable products or services to meet their customers' needs and increase customer loyalty. This approach involves dividing markets into segments or niches and then tailoring the company's offerings to meet the demands of those niches. Creating customer loyalty requires employees to combine detailed knowledge about their customers with operational flexibility so they can respond quickly to almost any customer need, from customizing a product to fulfilling special requests. Consulting, retail, and banking organizations often adopt this approach. Employees in primary contact with customers would likely receive particular attention due to their key role in obtaining customer intimacy.

Most service-quality experts say that hiring is not only the first, but also the most critical step in building a customer-oriented company.[29] Hiring active learners with good customer relations skills and emotional resilience under pressure would complement a competitive advantage based on customer intimacy, and help ensure that the organization continually enhances its ability to deliver on promises to customers.[30] Because employee cooperation and collaboration are important to developing customer intimacy, staffing efforts should also focus on identifying and attracting adaptable team players with good networking skills.

A discussion of Starbucks may help to highlight the importance of consistency between a company's staffing strategy and its business strategy. Starbucks is able to command a high price for a cup of coffee because it focuses on its relationship with customers. Imagine if Starbucks reduced its investment in its staffing function and began to hire cheaper labor, including people who don't enjoy interacting with customers, or people who have weak communication skills. Soon Starbucks' competitive advantage would begin to erode and its brand would lose its luster. Starbucks would have to reduce the price of its coffee to keep customers coming back. Eventually, Starbucks could find itself pursuing a cost-leadership strategy rather than a specialization strategy because it failed to recruit and hire the right types of people.

Growth Strategy

Another strategic choice is whether to expand the company and seek to increase business. Companies often pursue a growth strategy in response to investor preferences for rising earnings per share, and the required business expansion generally requires the acquisition of additional talent. For example, growth-oriented chains such as Starbucks regularly open new stores that require additional management, employees, and even product distribution staff.

The success of a growth strategy depends on the firm's ability to find and retain the right number and types of employees to sustain its intended growth. Growth can be *organic,* happening as the organization expands from within by opening new factories or stores. If it is, it requires an investment in recruiting, selecting, and training the right people to expand the company's operations. Firms can also pursue growth strategies through *mergers and acquisitions.* Mergers and acquisitions have been a common way for organizations to achieve growth, expand internationally, and respond to industry deregulation. In addition to expanding the organization's business, mergers and acquisitions can also be a way for an organization to acquire the quality and amount of talent it needs to execute its business strategy.

For example, an organization whose growth strategy requires it to hire thousands of additional experienced IT consulting specialists may seek to acquire a company that already employs this talent. It is not unusual for organizations to acquire other companies solely for their talent, and subsequently discontinue the business the acquired company was initially in. Employees in redundant positions or in jobs not needed by the merged organization are reassigned or let go and the targeted talent is incorporated into the acquiring company's ranks. Assuming the targeted talent stays with the merged organization, which is not guaranteed, this strategy can be effective in expanding an organization's talent base. It is important to consider the match between organization cultures, values, talent philosophy, and HR practices when using mergers and acquisitions as a way to implement a growth strategy. Mismatches between merged or acquired organizations can result in the loss of talented employees. Mergers and acquisitions often fail because of people issues rather than technical or financial issues.

Changing Business Strategy

Strategy implementation and strategic change require large-scale organizational changes, one of the largest of which may be the nature of the competencies, values, and experiences required of employees. Depending on the nature of a strategic change, some employees are likely to lack the willingness or even the ability to support the new strategy. Targeting staffing efforts to hire people who will be willing and able to implement a new strategy may help it to take hold and ultimately influence the strategy's effectiveness.

Imagine an organization currently manufacturing semiconductor chips. The competitive environment is such that the organization must compete on cost. The organization is focused on operational efficiencies to control expenses and tries to hire the best labor it can at the lowest wages possible. Its focus is on keeping hiring and training costs contained, and the organization promotes from within when possible to help achieve these goals. Now consider what would change if the organization identifies a better competitive position by specializing in designing new and innovative computer chips and outsourcing their production. The organization's recruiting focus would now be on identifying and attracting the best and brightest research and development talent to join the organization, and the cost of doing so would be less of a factor. External hires would be more prevalent despite their higher cost because the need for the top chip design skills necessitates a large investment in talent. The return on the larger staffing investment would be much greater than under the old low-cost producer strategy. Intel went through this type of transformation in the early 1970s when it moved from being a producer of semiconductor memory chips to programmable microprocessor chips.

Because staffing influences the skills, motivations, and interests of the organization's employees, unintended strategies may emerge in an organization as employees exercise their interests and skills. These emergent strategies can open new market opportunities and influence future business strategy. For example, an organization intending to become a leader in pharmaceutical drug research and development may alter its course toward genomics research because it finds that many of the scientists it has hired to do traditional research have skills and expertise in this area as well.

Organizational Life Cycle

The *organizational and product life cycle* can also influence a firm's choice of strategy. As a firm or a particular product ages, it grows, matures, declines, and dies. Strategies often change to adjust to the different needs of each stage in the life cycle. During the *introduction* stage when a company is forming, attracting top technical and professional talent is often a priority, often requiring the company to meet or exceed market compensation rates. If they lack the resources to pay what is required to attract the quality of talent they need to get their company off the ground, many companies give employees some sort of ownership in the company. During the *growth* stage, new companies or products must set themselves apart from competitors to gain customers and market share. Growth companies often pursue innovation or differentiation strategies to distinguish themselves from their competition. Because they are less established and thus higher-risk employers, they often need to invest more money and resources in staffing to attract the talent they need to grow. Because they lack a large and strong internal talent pool, and they need to add new employees as they grow, they frequently need to hire from outside the organization and tend to have an external talent focus. Because of their rapid growth, promotions and internal moves can be faster than during the other stages of an organization's life cycle.

During the *maturity* stage of a firm's life cycle, products and services have fully evolved, and the product's market share has become established. The focus now shifts to maintaining or obtaining further market share through cost leadership, often by streamlining operations and focusing on efficiency. Because mature companies have a larger pool of internal talent from which to draw, the talent focus becomes more internal. Because the company's growth often slows during the maturity stage, promotion opportunities may decrease unless turnover of lower performers is carefully managed. Many companies also restructure during their mature years, requiring employees to be more adaptable and mobile as the company's needs for workers and skills change.

Companies in *decline* are facing shrinking markets and weaker business performance. A company in decline can pursue a cost-leadership strategy and allow the decline to continue until the business is no longer profitable, or it can try to make changes to revive the product or service. If it chooses to try to change its product or service, the firm typically adopts a specialization or differentiation strategy.

Up to this point, we have discussed how a firm's business strategy shapes its staffing needs and influences the characteristics it looks for in new hires. A firm's HR strategy and its talent philosophy influence its staffing strategy. We next discuss talent philosophy in greater detail, followed by its role in shaping HR and staffing strategies.

Talent Philosophy

An organization's talent philosophy is a system of beliefs about how its employees should be treated. It reflects how an organization thinks about its employees, and is typically shaped by its founders. For example, some organizations view employees as partners and key stakeholders in the company, while others view employees as more expendable and easily replaceable. A company's business strategy can also influence how a company interacts with its employees, which then affects how it decides to manage the movement of people into, through, and out of the company.

HR strategy is the linkage of the entire HR function with the firm's business strategy and talent philosophy in order to improve business strategy execution. Strategic HR management aligns a company's values and goals with the behaviors, values, and goals of employees. An organization's HR strategy, in turn, influences the sub-strategies of each of the HR functions, including staffing, performance management, training, and compensation. The alignment of these separate functions creates an integrated HR management system supporting the execution of the business strategy, guided by the talent philosophy of the organization.

An organization's overall staffing strategy is the constellation of priorities, policies, and behaviors used to manage the flow of talent into, through, and out of an organization over time. An organization's talent strategy thus encompasses its approaches to acquiring, deploying, and retaining its talent, and the choice of jobs to which it devotes greater or lesser resources. A firm's staffing strategy ultimately reflects its business strategy, HR strategy, and talent philosophy. We next look more closely at how a company's talent philosophy shapes its staffing strategy.

If not created intentionally, a firm's talent philosophy develops on its own as the personal values of high-level managers are expressed in their hiring and talent management decisions and actions. Over time, these values and perspectives become those of the organization. Johnson & Johnson articulates its talent philosophy in part of its credo:

> We are responsible to our employees, the men and women who work with us throughout the world. Everyone must be considered as an individual. We must respect their dignity and recognize their merit. They must have a sense of security in their jobs. Compensation must be fair and adequate, and working conditions clean, orderly and safe. We must be mindful of ways to help our employees fulfill their family responsibilities. Employees must feel free to make suggestions and complaints. There must be equal opportunity for employment, development and advancement for those qualified. We must provide competent management, and their actions must be just and ethical.[31]

Table 3 contains several questions an organization's talent philosophy typically addresses. We will discuss each of the questions next.

Table 3. Questions Addressed by an Organization's Talent Philosophy

1. Do we want people to contribute to the company over long-term careers or do we want to focus on filling vacancies in the short term?
2. Do we value the ideas and contributions of people with diverse ideas and perspectives?
3. Do we see our employees as assets to be managed or as investors who choose where to allocate their time and efforts?
4. What are our ethical principles when it comes to our employees?

Filling Vacancies or Hiring for Long-Term Careers

An organization's talent philosophy can focus on a short- or long-term horizon. Some organizations fill open positions with people able to do the open job without considering their likelihood to advance to higher levels within the firm. Their only concern is getting a qualified person in the vacant job as soon as possible. Other organizations, including Nokia, believe in hiring people with the ability to perform the vacant job now, and the potential to move into other positions in the organization over time.

An organization's philosophy of filling vacancies or hiring for long-term careers is reflected in its staffing strategy. If a company's talent philosophy is to hire for long-term careers, it should focus on hiring people likely to be promoted and able to assume future leadership roles in the organization. This increases the likelihood that employees will be able to take advantage of the training and career advancement opportunities the organization makes available. It should also invest more heavily in the staffing system for entry-level positions, as this is also the source of the company's future leaders.

If a company intentionally has high turnover, the better strategic choice may be to focus on filling vacancies quickly and hiring people who can hit the ground running because any training costs are unlikely to be recovered if a new hire leaves quickly. If turnover is low and the company invests a lot of money and time developing employees, then the better strategic choice may be to hire for long-term careers. Similarly, if the company's business involves long-term projects or higher-level managers need substantial knowledge about how the company works to be effective, then hiring for long-term careers makes sense.

Commitment to Diversity

Another component of an organization's talent philosophy is its commitment to diversity. A firm can proactively recruit a diverse mix of people and strive to incorporate diversity into its workplace, or more passively let diversity happen on its own to the extent that it occurs. In light of the many laws and regulations covering staffing activities, as well as the fact that diversity has the potential to enhance organizational performance, actively managing diversity through staffing is usually the better strategic choice.

Diversity is important for more than legal reasons. Years of research have shown that well-managed, heterogeneous groups will generally outperform homogeneous groups in problem solving, innovation, and creative solution building, which are critical to business success in today's fast-paced global marketplace.[32] Organizations also benefit from diversity because their customers are diverse. In the United States today, black, Hispanic, Asian American, and Native American consumers have an estimated combined spending power of more than $1.3 trillion.[33] Diverse employees may be better able to understand and negotiate with different customers.

An organization's staffing strategy reflects its commitment to diversity. An organization proactively seeking diversity is likely to establish relationships with recruiting sources of diverse people and actively create a culture of inclusion. For example, law firm Mintz Levin's commitment to diversity is reflected in how it recruits. In addition to hosting an Annual Mock Interview Workshop for minority law students, it regularly participates in minority job fairs. Mintz Levin attorneys also mentor women and minority law students by speaking at diversity and recruiting symposia.[34]

Applicants and Employees as Assets or Investors

Another important way organizations differ in their talent philosophies is in viewing their job applicants and employees as either assets (i.e., "human capital") or as investors. If job applicants and employees are thought of as *assets*, the staffing focus is on managing costs and controlling the asset (as is the case with managing other assets such as land, equipment, or steel). As a result, the goal tends to focus on the acquisition and deployment of labor as cheaply and quickly as possible.

Alternatively, if applicants and employees are thought of as investors rather than expenses, the focus is on establishing a mutually beneficial relationship in which employees are recognized as investing their resources (time, talents, energy, etc.) in the organization in exchange for a return on that investment (supportive culture, pay, benefits, challenge, professional development, etc.). Because talented employees (as investors) can choose not to invest in the company (by not applying for or accepting a job) or to discontinue their investment in the organization (by leaving) at any time, an organization with this philosophy does its best to be as attractive as possible to potential and current employees. When viewing applicants and employees as investors, the goal is to give them a return on their personal investment in the organization.

An organization's staffing strategy reflects whether it looks at its employees as assets or investors. Viewing employees as an asset to be managed generally leads to a low-cost approach to staffing. A dominant staffing goal would be to acquire employees who can perform the duties of a job as quickly and as cheaply as possible. Recruitment sources and selection methods requiring a large amount of time or money would be less likely to be used than those producing candidates quickly and cheaply. Although an asset-based talent philosophy is unlikely to generate high employee commitment,[35] an asset approach to staffing and managing talent can be effective for organizations pursuing a low-cost strategy in which high levels of skill are not required and high levels of turnover are not disruptive or prohibitively expensive.

On the other hand, organizations relying on new product innovation—and for which the commitment and efforts of employees are key drivers of organizational performance, as is the case for research and development organizations such as Corning, Pfizer, Whirlpool, and Genentech—may find themselves handicapped by an asset philosophy of talent. A key driver of success for these companies is the motivation, commitment, and engagement of their employees. If an organization whose success is dependent on the creation of new products and technologies is unable to attract appropriately skilled employees and is unable to leverage its employees' full potential, then it will not perform as effectively as it could. Viewing employees as assets to be controlled is less likely to attract top talent and inspire their best performance.

Commitment to Ethical Behavior

An organization's philosophy toward ethical issues, including fairness, honesty, and integrity, is reflected in its talent philosophy and staffing strategy. A firm with a talent philosophy focused on maintaining high ethical standards is more likely to explain to applicants its hiring process, how it will make hiring decisions, and the reasons for all of the assessment methods used to evaluate job candidates. Communications with candidates are likely to be more frequent, and delays minimized. Rather than trying to build job applicants' and employees' trust, firms whose staffing philosophies are less focused on ethics might focus more on expediency and low cost.

Johnson & Johnson applies its core ethical values to how it staffs and manages the flow of its workforce. Its ethics and corporate values are reflected in its staffing philosophy of investing in the evaluation and development of its employees,[36] respectfully and honestly explaining its hiring process on its web site, and decentralized decision-making that allows each business unit control over its hiring decisions.

Professional guidelines exist to help organizations establish standards for staffing conduct. These guidelines are not laws, but recommendations made by government agencies and professional organizations and societies to address ethical issues and the many gray areas of the law. Staffing specialists are expected to adhere to these defined sets of professional standards. Some of the best sources for staffing-related standards and ethical guidelines are listed in Table 4.

Table 4. Sources for Staffing Standards and Ethical Guidelines

The American Psychological Association (APA)	Published a document that describes test takers' rights and responsibilities. (Available online at http://www.apa.org/science/ttrr.html.)
	Published the *Standards for Educational and Psychological Testing* (1999) along with the American Educational Research Association, American Psychological Association, and the National Council on Measurement in Education. (Available for purchase online at: http://www.apa.org/science/standards.html.)
	Publishes reports to address emerging staffing issues such as the APA's position on good and ethical Internet testing practice[i] and test user qualifications[ii]. (Many of these reports are free on the APA web site: http://www.apa.org/science/testing.html.)
	Published ethical guidelines to help staffing experts. (Available online at: http://www.apa.org/ethics/code2002.html.)
The Society for Industrial and Organizational Psychology (Division 14 of the American Psychological Association)	*Principles for the Validation and Use of Personnel Selection Procedures* (2003). (Available online at http://www.siop.org/_Principles/principlesdefault.aspx.)
	Published a report on recordkeeping and defining job applicants in Internet testing.[iii]
The Uniform Guidelines on Employee Selection Procedures (1978)	Although lacking coverage of Internet-related staffing issues, the Guidelines define discrimination and good conduct for validity studies and suggest ways for identifying adverse impact and ensuring the appropriateness of a staffing process. (Available online at: http://www.dol.gov/dol/allcfr/ESA/Title_41/Part_60-3/toc.htm.)
The Society for Human Resource Management (SHRM)	Represents more than 250,000 HR practitioners and provides numerous resources and publications on its web site (http://www.shrm.org). SHRM's code of ethics for its members is available online at: http://www.shrm.org/ethics/code-of-ethics.asp.
Academy of Management (1978)	Founded in 1936, it is a leading professional association for scholars dedicated to creating and disseminating knowledge about management and organizations (www.aom.pace.edu). The code of ethics for members can be found at: http://www.aomonline.org/aom.asp?id=14&page_id=235.

[i] Naglieri, J.A., et al, "Psychological Testing on the Internet: New Problems, Old Issues," *American Psychologist*, 2004, 59, pp. 150-62.
[ii] Turner, S.M., DeMers, S.T., Fox, H.R., & Reed, G.M. "APA's Guidelines for Test User Qualifications: An Executive Summary," *American Psychologist*, 2001, 56, pp. 1099-113.
[iii] Reynolds, D., "EEOC and OFCCP Guidance on Defining a Job Applicant in the Internet Age: SIOP's Response," *The Industrial-Organizational Psychologist*, 2004, 42, pp. 127-38.

Table 5 gives some examples of how a firm's staffing strategy is influenced by its HR strategy and talent philosophy.

Table 5. How Talent Philosophy Influences HR Strategy and Staffing Strategy

Talent Philosophy	HR Strategy	Staffing Strategy
Want employees to contribute to the firm over long-term careers.	Acquire, develop, and retain talent able to contribute to the firm over time.	*Hire:* Recruit and hire talent able to perform now and grow into future jobs. *Deploy:* Use succession planning, career planning, and career development to take advantage of employees' potential over time. *Retain:* Retain top performers and high-potential employees.
Value the ideas and contributions of people with diverse ideas and perspectives.	Acquire and retain a diverse workforce; create and maintain a culture of inclusion and respect to leverage diversity.	*Hire:* Recruit and hire diverse people and people comfortable with diversity. *Deploy:* Create mentoring programs. *Retain:* Reward and promote diversity champions.
View applicants and employees as investors of their time and effort.	Develop a mutually beneficial relationship with employees; respect applicants and employees and their other life and family responsibilities.	*Hire:* Attract and hire employees who fit the firm's culture and values; respond quickly to applicant inquiries. *Deploy:* Put employees in jobs that match their interests and abilities. *Retain:* Allow flexible work arrangements to meet employees' needs.
High ethical standards toward applicants and employees.	Treat applicants and employees with fairness, honesty, and integrity.	*Hire:* Explain the hiring decision process and the uses of all assessment methods; hire based on merit; comply with laws. *Deploy:* Give honest performance feedback. *Retain:* Promote based on merit.

Deriving Staffing Strategy

Strategy execution, rather than strategy choice, determines an organization's competitive success. Having an appropriate and high-potential strategy is useless unless it is executed, and execution is often the biggest strategic challenge for organizations. For example, when Lou Gerstner first became CEO of IBM, employees resisted the changes he tried to implement. He found that his biggest challenge was not deciding which direction to take the company, but figuring out how to execute his strategy.[37] Staffing is a key step toward strategy execution.

Business strategy execution ultimately depends on employees' willingness and ability to execute it. Leaders with a talent mind-set generally share Allied Signal CEO Larry Bossidy's conviction that, "At the end of the day, we bet on people, not strategies."[38] Such leaders believe that building their talent pool is a competitive advantage in itself, and is an important part of their job.

An organization's HR strategy links its entire HR function to the execution of the organization's business strategy.[39] It addresses the question of "how will the organization's talent acquisition and retention, training, compensation, and performance management functions contribute to the organization's competitive advantage and help it to successfully compete in its marketplace?" If a business wishes to pursue a low-cost strategy in its marketplace, it will need to focus on controlling labor costs, reducing expensive turnover, and hiring people willing to work for market or below-market wages. Its training programs would likely be streamlined to focus narrowly on currently needed behaviors and skills, and the performance management system would reward performance rather than innovation. This broader understanding of the role of the organization's HR systems and functions in supporting the business strategy then guides the development of a more specific strategy for each of the functional areas.

An organization's business strategy determines the types of people it needs to employ. Having the right people in key positions is one of the most fundamental aspects of a successful strategy.[40] There are direct recruitment and staffing implications of the business strategy an organization chooses to pursue. A job analysis can translate every job into a set of employee competencies, styles, and traits that enable job incumbents and the organization to perform the job and execute the company's business strategy. One of the key goals of hiring is to ensure that the people hired have the talents necessary to execute the business strategy. Doing this requires the determination of:

(1) the investment that needs to be made in staffing for each job;
(2) whether to recruit for desired skills for future jobs and roles or only the present job opening; and
(3) what levels of which current skills are needed in new hires. Identifying these and other goals establishes a critical link between the organization's business strategy and its HR (and staffing) function.

Unless employees are capable of setting and achieving appropriate personal goals relevant to the organization's strategy, other areas of competitive advantage may be useless.[41] Because different recruitment and selection practices attract and hire different types of individuals, the business strategy influences the staffing practices an organization needs. At a minimum, an organization's business strategy is likely to influence

(1) its talent philosophy;
(2) the type of people the organization recruits;
(3) the type of information communicated during the hiring process;
(4) the type of recruiter used; and
(5) the type of recruitment media used to publicize openings.[42]

An innovative firm like 3M, which values diversity, innovation, and long-term commitment by employees, focuses on attracting and hiring intelligent and intellectually curious individuals. 3M highlights the importance of diversity and its long history of commitment to innovation. As stated on its web site, "At 3M, our recruiting efforts are first and foremost dedicated to identifying talent. With that goal in mind, we look for individuals from all walks of life that share our commitment to innovation and excellence."[43]

An organization's staffing strategy should be derived from and be clearly supportive of its overall HR strategy. The strategies developed for each HR functional area should support the overall HR strategy. For example, RMB Holdings is the holding company of some of South Africa's leading financial services companies. Its HR strategy is to "recruit, build and retain the best people from South Africa's diverse population base. In particular, it seeks people with an entrepreneurial attitude and encourages an owner-manager culture. People are empowered, held accountable for their actions and are rewarded appropriately."[44]

McDonald's people are its most important asset. Its success depends on customer satisfaction, which begins with workers who have the attitudes and abilities required to work efficiently and provide good customer service. To execute its growth strategy, McDonald's has identified "People" as one of its three global corporate strategies for success. McDonald's states in its "People Vision" that as an employer it wants "to Be the Best Employer in Each Community Around the World."[45] It also makes a "People Promise" to its employees that "We Value You, Your Growth and Your Contributions."[46] Its five "People Principles" that reflect its HR strategy are: respect and recognition; values and leadership behaviors; competitive pay and benefits; learning, development, and personal growth; and ensuing that employees have the resources needed to get the job done.[47]

As another example, here is the stated HR strategy for Metso, an organization whose core businesses are fiber and paper technology, rock and mineral processing, and automation and control technology:

> The aim of Metso's human resource strategy is to ensure the availability of skilled and committed personnel needed by Metso's businesses and to develop such human resource policies that allow utilizing the intellectual capital in achieving common goals. The goals of the human resource strategy further involve directing the transformation in Metso

towards a new type of knowledge environment, staying up-to-date with the surrounding world and anticipating changes affecting human resource policies.

The role of the human resource function is to safeguard the development of knowledge and competencies, as well as the development of leadership required for a motivating working atmosphere and the desired personnel structure. The tasks of the human resource function further involve providing support to networking and establishment of sustainable ways of operation. Moreover, we ensure for our part that Metso is an attractive and respected employer to both existing and future Metso professionals.[48]

The primary staffing strategies for both of these organizations (McDonald's and Metso) are easily derived from their broader HR strategies. Because staffing activities are not the only HR activities an organization undertakes, it is also important that the strategies of each functional area of human resources complement each other as well as the organization's higher-level HR strategy. For example, a staffing strategy of hiring people with the potential to fill higher-level positions over time would be unlikely to work without well-designed and implemented training and development systems.

Strategic Staffing Decisions

A company's talent philosophy reflects how it thinks about its employees. It also influences its staffing strategy, which is the set of priorities, policies, and behaviors the company uses to manage the flow of talent into, through, and out of an organization over time. Organizations make several decisions in developing and executing their staffing strategies. The nine decisions that influence a company's staffing strategy are summarized in Table 6.

Table 6. Nine Elements of Staffing Strategy

1. Do we want a core or flexible workforce?
2. Do we prefer to hire internally or externally?
3. Do we want to hire for or train and develop needed skills?
4. Do we want to replace or retain our talent?
5. What levels of which skills do we need?
6. Will we staff proactively or reactively?
7. Which jobs should we focus on?
8. Is staffing treated as an investment or a cost?
9. Will staffing be centralized or decentralized?

Should We Establish a Core or Flexible Workforce?

An organization's core workforce consists of people who are perceived by the organization to be regular employees of the organization who are central to what the organization does or produces. These workers are considered to be important, longer-term contributors to the company, and the company tries to retain them for long periods.

Flexible workers, or contingent workers, have less job security than the core workforce. They may be temporary, leased, part-time, or contract workers and typically have a formal contract with the organization that specifies the nature of their relationship. When business contracts, flexible workers are let go before core workers. When business expands, flexible workers may be added before core workers until it seems that the expansion will be permanent. A flexible workforce allows a company to quickly adjust to volatility in demand for its products or services and decreases the likelihood that layoffs from its core workforce will be necessary.

Companies such as Kelly Services, Accountemps, and Manpower provide temporary workers on an as-needed basis to help the firm adjust its workforce to its production needs. Eighty percent of employers use some form of nontraditional staffing arrangement, and many use more than one.[49] McDonnell Douglas (now Boeing) and Georgia-Pacific have used contingent workers as a key part of their staffing strategies.[50] Mail-order companies and shipping companies such as UPS and Federal Express regularly use temporary workers to ramp up for busy holiday periods.

Flexible arrangements can also help to meet the needs of the company's workforce. Although some flexible workers would prefer to be core workers and have greater job stability, flexible work arrangements allow many people to better balance their work and nonwork responsibilities such as school and family. Because some would be unable to work at all, having a flexible workforce can help an organization tap underutilized, high-quality labor pools. Flexible work arrangements often give workers greater flexibility and higher pay, although benefits such as health insurance and retirement contributions may be lower or nonexistent

Organizations need to determine which jobs are best for core and flexible workers, as well as the appropriate mix of core and flexible workers in each job. Support functions such as clerical workers are often better for flexible workers than jobs more central to the organization's strategic execution. Jobs central to what the organization does or produces typically contain more core workers, but may be filled by some temporary workers to protect the core workers from business fluctuations and layoffs.

Should Our Talent Focus Be Internal or External?

One aspect of an organization's talent philosophy concerns its preference for developing, retaining, and promoting employees, which is an internal talent focus, versus hiring new employees for higher-level jobs, which is an external talent focus. Which is the better choice? The answer depends on the organization's business strategy, talent philosophy, the quality of its employee assessment, training, and development programs, and the quality and cost of available talent. A biotechnology organization pursuing a business strategy of continually innovating new products that requires leading-edge technology requires a continual influx of recently educated and trained talent. As a result, it might want employees to stay with it for only a few years. Focusing on hiring people from outside the company would help it continually acquire the fresh talent with skills in the most recent technologies. On the other hand, a firm with a customer service strategy might need to retain long-term employees who have developed relationships with customers and an understanding of how the company can best meet their needs. Because it can lead to high turnover and an inability to create and maintain quality customer relationships, an external talent focus could undermine a customer service strategy.

Some organizations focus on developing their own talent and promoting from within rather than hiring new employees for higher-level jobs. Hiring people with the potential to learn and eventually assume leadership positions, succession planning, and career development help to ensure a supply of internal leadership talent. Both internal and external talent focuses can be effective depending on the organization's strategies and needs, and most companies use a mixed strategy that includes both internal and external hiring. A company's staffing strategy may be to consider internal candidates first, and if it cannot find a suitable internal person, then turn its attention to the outside. Alternatively, an internal and external search may be engaged simultaneously, with preference being given to internal candidates.

An internal talent focus requires hiring people with the capability to perform well in currently open positions as well as the potential to perform well in the organization's training and development programs and to eventually assume leadership positions in the organization. It also requires an investment in training and employee development to ensure a sufficient pool of qualified internal job candidates. An external talent focus often requires paying a premium to acquire talent with the existing skills and experience to perform well in the organization's currently open positions as the organization usually provides limited training. If the firm cannot find appropriate talent outside the firm, it will have to develop and promote from within, find a way to substitute technology for the scarce skills, or do without those skills. Table 7 summarizes reasons organizations pursue each focus.

Should We Hire for or Train Needed Skills?

Another strategic staffing decision is whether the organization prefers to hire people who already possess the desired skills and competencies to perform the job or whether it is willing to hire people without those skills and train them instead. McDonald's founder Ray Kroc once said, "If we are going to go anywhere, we've got to have talent. And, I'm going to put my money in talent."[51] Supporting this philosophy, McDonald's created a worldwide management training center called Hamburger University, which has trained more than 80,000 McDonald's managers since its founding in 1961.[52]

Companies unable to pay market wages for a particular job and thus unable to attract skilled workers may find it necessary to hire people willing and able to learn the job and train them instead. For jobs that are unique to an organization, skilled workers may not exist, making it necessary to hire trainable people and put them through a company-developed training program. If a company does not have an appropriate training budget or program, if there is no time to train new hires, or if the job needs to be filled immediately, the better decision would be to hire people already able to do the job who can hit the ground running.

Should Talent Be Replaced or Retained?

Organizations can choose to try to minimize turnover or accept whatever turnover happens and hire replacements as openings occur. The advantages of letting turnover occur and focusing on replacement include a more frequent infusion of new ideas and talent, which can

Table 7. Internal and External Talent Focuses

Reasons some organizations prefer to hire internally whenever possible:	• Because internal hiring sends employees the message that loyalty and good performance can be rewarded with a promotion, it can thus enhance employee motivation and retention. • One promotion could lead to additional internal promotions to fill the jobs left vacant. • Because greater information is known about candidates who already work for the organization, a more accurate assessment about candidates' fit with the job and organization can be made. • Internal hires will get up-to-speed in the new job faster because they are already familiar with the organization. • Jobs can be filled faster. • The return on the company's investment in training lower-level employees can be increased because more of them are ultimately promoted. • Higher training and development expenses associated with a focus on internal hiring may be offset by lower recruiting and hiring expenses and lower turnover costs. • Smaller or lesser-known organizations may have a difficult time attracting their desired level of talent externally. • Organizations with a strong, positive organizational culture may find that internal hires reinforce and strengthen that culture more so than external hires.
Reasons some organizations prefer to focus on external hiring:	• A lack of qualified internal candidates. • External hiring can enhance organizational diversity. • Focusing on external hires can increase the size and quality of the candidate pool. • External hires can inject new ideas and perspectives into the organization. • The cost of developing and maintaining internal training and development programs is greater than the hiring cost of external hires. • Smaller organizations may not have the internal talent that makes internal promotions feasible. • Internal promotions can be disruptive as multiple positions must be filled (because the promotion leads to additional inside promotions to fill the jobs left vacant) rather than only one position. • Too much internal movement can create instability and cause delays in project completion.

be useful for companies in fast-changing industries. For example, some biotechnology or computer software companies may find that their employees' talents are obsolete within a few years. Unless they are willing to invest in retraining their employees, it may be beneficial to encourage them to leave after a few years and replace them with new graduates trained in the latest technology. Focusing on replacement may also be less expensive than retention for jobs with an abundant labor supply. Advantages of retaining workers include a more loyal and committed workforce with a better understanding of the company's products, services, and processes, and decreased staffing costs. If a position is of particular importance to the running of the company, or if the talent needed by a particular position is difficult to find, focusing on retention can help to ensure that the position is not vacant any longer than is necessary.

What Levels of Which Skills Should We Seek?

One of the most critical staffing decisions concerns the types of skills a new hire should possess and the appropriate level of those skills. Although hiring managers often request "top talent," most jobs do not require top skills in all areas. Performing a job analysis to objectively analyze the job to determine exactly what is required for an incumbent to perform well is key in making this determination.

Some organizations' staffing goal is to hire only the individuals with the highest ability. To do this, the organization must first be able to recruit high-ability individuals and then be able to identify and hire the highest-ability applicants. For many organizations, this is an extremely difficult goal, because a limited number of high-ability people exists. Although this approach can be very appropriate for some organizations, such as top consulting firms or other businesses relying on knowledge workers to create new products, it is not the best approach for many organizations.

It is often more strategic to try to identify worker attributes that contribute to job success and business strategy execution, that are difficult to change through training, and that effectively differentiate among applicants. It is logical and cost-effective to identify those job-related attitudes and attributes that are difficult to change through training and hire people who already possess them. For example, technology services company EDS has a saying that they "hire the traits and train the skills."[53]

It is also important to determine whether a job should be filled by someone with only the skills needed to perform the job well today or whether there are additional competencies or characteristics that may be needed by the new hire to enable him or her to perform the job well in the future. In a rapidly changing business environment, focusing on current skills is insufficient. Employees need to also learn quickly, adapt to change, communicate effectively, and work well with others. Some jobs stay the same for long periods of time and others change rapidly. For the sake of long-term job success, it is helpful to consider what the next incumbent in a position needs to be able to do to perform the job successfully for a reasonable period and then hire someone with those skills. Even clerical jobs, which we often don't think of as rapidly changing, went through a period of rapid change when computers and word processing became mainstream. For many organizations, manual typewriter skills became obsolete in a period of just a few years and word processing and software skills became critical. Hiring an office assistant skilled only in manual typing when an office was about to adopt computer technology would not be as strategic as hiring an office assistant able to use both a typewriter and a computer.

Should We Pursue Proactive or Reactive Staffing?

Proactive staffing is done before situations or issues come up, rather than in response to them, as is the case with reactive staffing. An organization can staff its positions proactively or reactively in regards to diversity, as well as talent quality. Proactive diversity decisions would include recruiting from sources known to be diverse, tracking the diversity of hires produced by each recruiting source, and constantly monitoring progress toward diversity goals. Reactive diversity decisions occur when a specific event, such as being sued for hiring discrimination, prompts the organization to take a closer look at its staffing practices. Reactive organizations take a more "wait-and-see" approach to staffing, while proactive organizations try to identify practices or situations that could be problematic and work to improve them before they become problems.

Organizations typically recruit when they need to fill a specific job opening, which is job-oriented staffing. However, when labor markets are tight and good recruits are hard to find, organizations must pursue talent-oriented staffing and pursue scarce talent constantly—not just when a vacancy occurs. This alternative philosophy promotes the identification of where the firm's future skill gaps are going to be well in advance of actual needs, then the generation of a continuous talent stream into the staffing pipeline to ensure there are always qualified people in various stages of the hiring process. For example, because of the nursing shortage in many areas of the country, some hospitals are partnering with local high schools, and Johnson & Johnson developed a media campaign to generate interest in the nursing profession.

Some firms create unique or *idiosyncratic* jobs for people with talents the organization can put to use. Idiosyncratic jobs are created around a current or new employee's unique experience, knowledge, skills, interests, and abilities.[54] Rather than focusing on whether there is currently an opening before evaluating available talent, the person is hired and then a job is created to exploit the individual's strengths. For example, when someone steps down from a position in the White House, it is common for a consulting or lobbying firm to hire them in a "consulting" role to take advantage of their connections.

An additional advantage of a talent-oriented talent philosophy is that it can speed up the hiring process and decrease the amount of time jobs stay unfilled. With qualified job candidates already in the advanced stages of the hiring process, hiring is faster when a position opens. Because more time is taken to generate qualified job candidates, a deeper pool of candidates is usually created from which to choose the moment a position opens. This can be a better strategic choice than the traditional job-oriented approach used by most organizations of waiting for a position to open, posting a job vacancy for a specified period of time, waiting for job applicants to contact the organization in response, screening them, and then hoping that a suitable number of qualified candidates will be found.

At The Container Store in Dallas, store managers are required to invest two to three hours per week interviewing job candidates to help the company attain its goal of never having to place a job ad anywhere. Pre-screened job candidates exist before the next job opening is created. By maintaining a roster of qualified candidates to call on, even when seasonal employees need to be hired, the home office's two-person recruiting staff does not need to get involved.[55]

Whether an organization's talent philosophy is talent-oriented or job-oriented influences its staffing strategy. A talent-oriented talent philosophy often requires organizations to recruit regionally or nationally, and to assess how candidates can meaningfully contribute to the company rather than evaluating candidates against pre-defined job requirements. A job-oriented philosophy has a better chance of attracting the active, local job seeker who is considering a job change or is currently unemployed than attracting the top talent who could really add value to the organization but is currently working at a company located in another state.[56]

Staffing can also be considered to have a proactive or reactive role in the organization depending on the degree to which staffing issues are considered as input into the business strategy. If the business strategy is developed without considering staffing issues, staffing is reactive. If staffing issues, including opportunities and limitations, are considered while the business strategy is being developed and can influence the business strategy, then staffing decisions are being made proactively and strategically.

Which Jobs Should We Focus On?

Another component of a successful talent strategy is the identification of key jobs on which to focus additional attention and resources because of their importance to the company's performance and to the execution of its business strategy. All jobs do not warrant equal investment in recruitment or staffing activities. A company's key jobs are those that in some way create value for the organization by contributing to the generation or retention of clients' business or generating new capabilities or products for the organization. Whenever there is performance variability across people working in the same position, there is the potential to improve that position's contribution to the organization by raising the average performance level of those employees. For example, if some salespeople sell substantially more of a company's product than do others, staffing (as well as training) improvements may be identified that result in the hiring of a greater number of higher-performing salespeople and fewer lower-performing salespeople.

Firms must identify which capabilities are the most critical to establishing and maintaining a competitive advantage. An organization's capabilities include human resources, manufacturing, engineering, research and development, marketing, and management information systems. It must then identify which jobs and roles are critical to this competitive advantage. Focusing on better staffing the identified positions should help the company execute its business strategy and enhance its competitive advantage. If Federal Express executives are asked which would have a greater impact on profitability, a 15 percent improvement in their pilots or a 15 percent improvement in their couriers, they will identify the couriers. This illustrates the fact that it is not necessarily the employees who are paid the most money who deserve the most attention; it is the employees who are a key component of value creation.[57]

Imagine a group of Dell Computer customer service representatives responsible for answering customers' questions about the company's products and solving product problems. This is a key position because it is responsible for marketing the company's products and keeping customers satisfied with their purchase. Some of the customer service representatives are extremely effective at communicating with callers to understand their issues, providing clear and correct answers and solutions. Other customer service representatives are much less effective, taking much longer to understand callers' questions and problems, and often providing incorrect or ineffective answers and solutions. Callers to these lower-performing customer service representatives are more unhappy with the company's inability to address their needs and are less likely to buy the product again or recommend it to others than are callers speaking to the higher-performing representatives.

Because this is a key position that creates wealth for Dell by generating and retaining business, its staffing practices are worth the investment. If Dell can improve its staffing system to better recruit and select customer service representatives who will be more effective, it is more likely to retain callers as customers, experience better word-of-mouth, and generate additional business. If the average productivity of the customer service representatives also increases as a result of the new staffing system, fewer customer service representatives may be needed, saving the company money without compromising performance.

Is Staffing an Investment or a Cost?

It is not uncommon for an organization's average cost-per-hire to be many thousands of dollars. The *PricewaterhouseCoopers Saratoga 2005/2006 Human Capital Index Report* states the average organization spent 48 days and $3,270 to fill an open position. Staffing activities can obviously be expensive, but it is not appropriate to view the expense purely as a cost to be minimized. Investments in recruiting, staffing, and retention can lead to financial returns in terms of higher performance and productivity, stronger future leaders, lower training costs, and lower recruiting and staffing expenditures due to fewer vacancies. Just as effective investments in marketing and advertising can lead to a larger and more profitable customer base, investments in sourcing and recruiting can generate a greater number of higher-quality job applicants who are interested in joining and contributing to the company.

Unfortunately, many organizations view staffing as a cost and seek to minimize the expense associated with finding, attracting, and selecting new hires. If there can be meaningful performance differences across workers in the same job, staffing is a good investment. Consider a study of Bell Labs' star performers that found an eight-to-one difference between the productivity of stars and average computer programmers.[58] Even in jobs of medium complexity such as sales clerks and mechanics, a top performer is 12 times more productive than those at the bottom and 85 percent more productive than an average performer. In the most complex jobs such as insurance salespeople and account managers, a top performer is 127 percent more productive than an average performer.[59] For most companies, investing a little more money recruiting, hiring, and retaining better employees is likely to lead to a good return if the new system results in the consistent hiring of star employees. Effectively matching staffing strategies with the competencies, styles, values, and traits required by the positions being filled can save money, reduce the time required to fill positions because the search is more focused, improve the performance of employees, and even decrease turnover.

Although a staffing system should be thought of as an investment, this is not to say that cost is unimportant. Organizations must strike a balance between long-run investment and short-term cost containment. Most companies, particularly smaller ones, cannot pay unlimited amounts for optimal staffing systems, and return on investment must be considered along with the affordability of the initial staffing system investment for the organization.

To illustrate the possible return on investment for a staffing system, assume an organization has to hire 1,000 salespeople in the next year and that it has a choice of two different staffing systems. Both systems have similar but not identical capabilities. One system costs $900,000 while another costs $1.3 million. Because HR expenditures are typically treated as a cost in accounting systems, many managers and businesses would opt for the cheaper system. But which system is the better strategic choice? Assume the latter system generates employees who average $10,000 more in sales per employee per year than the cheaper system and 30 percent of those sales are profit. In the very first year the $400,000 investment in the more expensive staffing system would yield $3 million more in profit ($10,000*0.3*1,000), before taxes. This simple example illustrates how decisions may differ when viewing staffing as an investment rather than as an expense.

Technology and a looser labor market can reduce the average hiring cost for an organization. However, hiring costs at most companies are still a considerable investment. Maximizing the return on that investment requires that the staffing function prioritize its goals and make appropriate tradeoffs among them. Treating a staffing system as an investment rather than merely as a cost is likely to lead to different recruiting and staffing goals and outcomes.

Importantly, staffing systems also have the potential to enhance employee retention.[60] Any benefits from better staffing thus last over the longer tenure of the new hires, further increasing the return on the initial investment. These are not pie-in-the-sky numbers. Research has shown that higher-quality employees can generate even larger dollar-value differences in performance than in our illustration.[61] In the illustration, the more expensive system is clearly the better strategic choice (although this may not always be the case). The cost of the system is not what is most important. The most important issue for determining return on investment is the ability of the system to identify and recruit the right employees who stay with the organization long enough to allow the organization to recover the additional expense.

Should Our Staffing Function Be Centralized or Decentralized?

Who should manage the staffing process? This is a key aspect of a firm's staffing philosophy. A staffing function is *centralized* when an organization that has multiple business units has one staffing unit that is responsible for meeting at least some of the needs of all of the company's business units. Each business informs the centralized staffing function when it needs to hire, and the staffing unit then sources, recruits, and pre-screens candidates. The local business unit is still responsible for making a final hiring decision from the group of candidates or finalists sent to it by the staffing unit.

Centralized staffing, sometimes called *shared services staffing*, allows for greater economies of scale by channeling all of an organization's staffing activities through one unit. Duplication of work is minimized, which leads to greater efficiency and consistency. Multiple positions can be filled from the same candidate pool, and best practices are leveraged across the organization. Centralization enables resources to be quickly reallocated to meet changing business priorities and generally provides policies and procedures that offer some level of uniformity for the organization. This structure can also strengthen an organization's employer brand and image as an employer by ensuring consistency in how the organization presents itself and its job opportunities.

Decentralized staffing occurs when the different business units of a company each house their own staffing functions. It has the advantage of greater customer contact and more localized control over recruiting and staffing activities. This local specialization can improve recruiters' understanding of what type of person will be most successful in the particular unit. This structure gives staffing professionals greater flexibility to source and recruit in the best way for their location and labor market. A decentralized staffing function is more responsive to hiring managers because the staffing specialists report directly to them. Staffing metrics are less likely to be tracked or consolidated. Due to the lower volume of hires, and the duplication of effort across units, the result is higher costs.

Some organizations use a combination of centralized and decentralized approaches. Some areas of the staffing function are shared, and others are decentralized and tailored to meet the needs of each business unit. The combined approach can maximize each business unit's flexibility while standardizing the staffing metrics used throughout the company, minimizing redundancies, and leveraging technology and best practices. A combined approach can also help to build a more credible and productive relationship with hiring managers by giving hiring managers more discretion in local hiring processes than they would have under a centralized structure.

To bring in new partners, Starbucks implemented a staffing strategy that is both centralized and decentralized. According to Sheri Southern, vice president of partner resources for Starbucks North America, Starbucks' staffing strategy is, "To have the right people hiring the right people." Experienced store managers often make initial contact with potential recruits in the stores and at job fairs. Word-of-mouth and the company web site are also used to generate leads. Hiring managers are given hiring guidelines containing questions that help reveal whether recruits have the core competencies necessary for the job. The company also encourages recruits to self-select out of the hiring process by clearly stating in its hiring advertisements and on its web site that it wants people who are adaptable, dependable, and passionate team players. Starbucks also maintains a database of hundreds of thousands of online candidates who have answered preliminary informational and skills-based questions. This gives the company a head start on the hiring process, allowing it to staff more quickly.[62]

At Hewitt Associates, a provider of HR outsourcing and consulting, although recruiting activity is decentralized, business-unit recruiters have access to a variety of data and resources at the central office. The central office is used for policies, sourcing strategies, metrics, and consultation advice, if needed. But because they are dedicated to a particular business unit, the recruiters have a richer understanding of the business and skills for which they are recruiting.[63]

Competitive Talent Advantage

An organization's talent can create a competitive advantage by influencing the quality of the organization's stock of talent or the superiority of its work processes.[64] Resource stock and process capabilities reflect the difference between human capital advantage and human process advantage. The organization can generate human capital advantage by hiring and retaining outstanding people, producing a stock of exceptional talent.

Human process advantage is derived from superiority in how work gets done, and may be thought of as a function of complex processes that evolve over time, such as learning, cooperation, and innovation, which are very difficult to imitate.[65] For example, some firms may have very smart and capable managers (high-quality talent stock) but fail to fully use their talents as a result of excessive politics and infighting between departments (poor work processes). A competitive talent advantage can thus be thought of as organizations having a better stock of employees working with better processes.

Because a competitive advantage results from unique configurations of resources accumulated over time and by organizational processes that give rise to consistent performance differences, staffing can influence an organization's competitive advantage by shaping the characteristics of its workforce. Accordingly, staffing practices can create value for a firm when they result in greater efficiencies in productivity or labor costs, or when they positively impact customers' perceptions of the company's products and services.

Getting the right people on board *before* they are needed can prevent them from being hired by the competition and also ensure that appropriate talent will be available when the organization needs it. It may also result in better hires as you have more time to recruit than if you have a more immediate need. For example, Praxair believed that it could not afford to wait for the firm's future growth to finance its human resources. It considered new talent acquisition and employee development to be leading investments, and felt that the appropriate talent had to be in place before the company could be successful.[66]

Given that any competitive advantage erodes over time as competitors respond, an organization must do what it can to defend its current competitive advantage and regularly initiate new strategic initiatives to maintain its competitive position. Such activities can include broadening the company's product line or customer support (e.g., offer free or low-cost training to product users), patenting alternative technologies, further reducing costs and prices, and acquiring talent ahead of present needs to keep them from potential competitors. Even if an organization does not need more employees to meet its current labor demand, if it continues to acquire the top talent in its core competencies, it can both build its own internal talent pool and keep this top talent from competitors. Economic downturns often make excellent times for organizations to build up their talent reserves as the looser labor market makes it easier to hire good people at an affordable cost. When an industry is in an upswing, the labor pool becomes tighter and the competition for talent heats up.

Table 8 illustrates the staffing implications of the different sources of competitive advantage.

Table 8. Staffing Implications of Different Sources of Competitive Advantage

Source of Competitive Advantage	Description	Staffing Implications
Operational Excellence (Low Cost)	• Focus is on the efficient production and delivery of products and/or services • Objective is to lead industry in both price and convenience	• Efficiency focus • Adaptable • Trainable • Willing to follow standardized procedures
Product Leadership (Innovation)	• Provide continuous stream of new cutting-edge products and services • Objective is the fast commercialization of new ideas	• Top research talent • Entrepreneurial mind-set • Creativity • High tolerance for ambiguity • Interested in and motivated by learning and discovery
Customer Intimacy (Customization)	• Tailor and shape products and services to fit each customer's needs • Objective is long-term customer loyalty and long-term customer profitability	• Adaptable • Learning-oriented • Networking skills • Customer-relations skills • Emotional resilience

Goals of Strategic Staffing

Identifying Staffing Goals

Creating hiring goals that are clearly linked to organizational strategies and objectives guides the strategic staffing process. Strategic staffing should result in the organization being better able to execute its business strategy. *Process goals* relate to the hiring process itself, including how many of what quality applicants apply, attracting appropriate numbers of diverse applicants, and meeting hiring timeline goals such as completing interviews within two weeks and making job offers within one week of the final interview. *Outcome goals* apply to the product of the hiring effort and include the number and quality of people hired, the financial return on the staffing investment, and whether the staffing effort improved organizational effectiveness. Table 9 presents a sampling of the many possible staffing goals.

Not all of these goals may be relevant for every hiring situation, and different goals are likely to take priority at different times. It is also common for staffing goals to conflict. For example, it can be challenging to hire top performers who will stay with the organization for many years while simultaneously filling jobs quickly and minimizing staffing costs.

Firms that do not staff strategically are often focused on goals such as the time it takes to fill an opening, the number of hires a recruiter produces in a period of time, and the cost-per-hire. Although these can be useful goals for improving the *efficiency* of the staffing process, they are not necessarily aligned with improving the *strategic performance* of the staffing system.

If strategy execution requires top-tier talent, recruitment goals should emphasize applicant quality and prioritize it above hiring speed. Because jobs change and different technologies are introduced, the people best able to do a job as it exists today may be less able to do the job in a few years. The development of a sound staffing strategy first requires the identification of the key objectives of the staffing effort,[67] which may change over time and be different for different positions.

Table 9. Examples of Staffing Goals[i]

Process Goals	• Attracting sufficient numbers of appropriately qualified applicants • Complying with the law and any organizational policies (e.g., anti-nepotism rules) • Fulfilling any affirmative action obligations • Meeting hiring timeline goals (e.g., hiring within one month of a job requisition approval) • Staffing efficiency
Outcome Goals	• Hiring individuals who succeed in their jobs • Hiring individuals who will eventually be promoted • Hiring individuals who will stay with the organization for a reasonable period of time • Hiring individuals likely to succeed in the firm's training and development programs • Meeting stakeholder needs • Maximizing the financial return on the organization's staffing investment • Enhancing the diversity of the organization • Enabling organizational flexibility • Enhancing business strategy execution

[i] Breaugh, J.A. (1992). *Recruitment: Science and practice.* Boston: PWS-Kent Publishing Company; HRMetrics.org, "Metrics," Available online at: http://hrmetrics.org/Metrics/index.asp. Accessed June 28, 2008; Weddle, P.D., "Take a Relevant Look at New-Hire Success," CareerJournal.com. Available online at: http://www.careerjournal.com/hrcenter/weddlesguide/20040405-weddle177.html. Accessed June 28, 2008.

The primary goal of staffing is to match the competencies, styles, values, and traits of job candidates with the requirements of the organization and its jobs. Strategic staffing goes even further and enables the organization to better execute its strategy and attain its goals. Each organization's staffing goals are likely to be different because different organizations pursue different business strategies. Furthermore, differences usually exist in a single organization's staffing goals across positions and over time because positions change and different positions require different talents.

For some positions, hiring top talent that is likely to stay with the organization for a long time may be critical (perhaps in management, long-term research and development projects, or sales). There may be other positions in the same organization for which average talent with moderate turnover is acceptable (perhaps administrative help). Each organization needs to identify for itself what its staffing goals are for any position, recognizing that its goals may change over time as the organization changes its strategy or faces changes in its labor or product markets. These goals should be based on the priorities of the organization as well as the needs of the hiring managers. Table 10 contains some key questions to ask in setting strategic staffing goals.

Table 10. Questions to Ask in Setting Staffing Goals

- Is it more important to fill the position quickly or with someone who closely matches a particular talent profile?
- What levels of which competencies, styles, values, and traits are really needed for job success and to execute the business strategy?
- What is the business strategy and what types of people will be needed in one, five, and 10 years to effectively execute it?
- What are the talents that new hires must have that we cannot train or otherwise make up for?
- What are the organization's long-term talent needs? Is it important that the people we hire for this job have the potential to assume leadership roles in the future?

It is also important to ensure that the goals of the staffing effort are consistent with the goals and needs of other stakeholders, including the individual hiring manager to whom the new hire will report. Each work group and supervisor differs in the type of person who would be best able to perform well in the job and work environment. Identifying these differences is important to making the staffing effort a success. One of the key roles of the recruiter is partnering with the hiring manager to assess his or her underlying needs and clearly define the competencies, values, and experiences being recruited in light of the reality of the job and work unit. For example, if web site development is being outsourced, then additional web site development skills may not be what the hiring manager really needs even if an employee with these skills has recently left. Jobs change, and the needs and talent mixes of work groups change, so it is important to reassess each position rather than rely on the same job description for every position opening. New hires should also fit the supervising manager's leadership style and the culture of the workgroup. Because hiring managers may not recognize changing talent needs or really know what they need in a new hire, hiring managers should see recruiters as partners in this process.

Hiring for retention and planned "churn" of employees can also be relevant to an organization. In some cases, particularly when technology is changing rapidly, organizations prefer to maintain a steady supply of new hires whose skills are as current as possible rather than relying on continual re-training of existing employees. If the skill sets of employees who have been with the company for several years are inferior to those of new hires recently trained in current technologies, planning for regular churn is a better strategic choice.

For example, a small software development firm that does not have a lot of money to invest in training may feel that an appropriate goal is to replace most of its programmers every two to four years and offer two-year contracts to its workers. Other organizations, like SAS, the world's largest privately held software company, may value long employee tenure with the company and prefer to invest in ongoing employee development. If building and maintaining customer relationships is important, and if unique organizational knowledge is critical for getting the organization's work done, or if the organization plans to develop its future leaders from within, then a more appropriate staffing goal may be a reduction in turnover.

Other possible staffing goals may be important for organizations using work teams, including continuous learning, employee willingness to help others, and workforce adaptability. If an organization's environment is changing rapidly and the organization must remain flexible if it is to successfully compete, its focus may be on hiring people who can learn and adapt quickly to new technologies and ideas, and share what they learn with other employees. It is important to remember that hiring only for the skill set appropriate for a job as it exists today may not be as strategic as hiring someone who is also able to learn new skills quickly and readily adapt to change. Organizations are wise to consider not just the current requirements for a position, but future requirements as well, and to incorporate both into their staffing goals.

The ultimate goal for a staffing system is to hire people who can perform well, contribute to the execution of the company's business strategy, and increase profits. Doing so as quickly as possible and experiencing a good return on the time and resources invested in the staffing effort are also important. Staffing goals should be identified in the early stages of staffing planning, and the staffing system should be evaluated to ensure that it is meeting these goals.

Many resources exist to help staffing professionals stay current and informed. Table 11 describes several Internet staffing resources.

Evaluating the Staffing System

Linking the goals of a staffing effort directly to the evaluation criteria the firm will use in assessing the staffing system's success is key to the effective evaluation of the success of a staffing system. For example, if filling positions quickly is an important goal, then the time it takes to fill each position should be tracked and evaluated for each recruiting source. However, it should be recognized that filling positions quickly may require tradeoffs against the quality of the talent pool that will be quickly accessible. If maintaining high-quality applicants is also an important goal, then the quality of recruits from different recruiting sources should also be tracked and evaluated. Because staffing goals should be closely aligned with the organization's business strategy, it is important to ensure that the goals are being met.

Table 11. Internet Staffing Resources

There are many resources available on the Internet that provide additional information and resources for staffing professionals. They include

The Equal Employment Opportunity Commission (www.eeoc.gov)	Provides information about the laws enforced by the EEOC and compliance guidance.
Electronic Recruiting Exchange (ere.net)	Has information and articles related to recruiting and employer branding.
Hrmetrics.org	Contains information about and examples of recruiting and staffing metrics.
Human Resource Planning Society (hrps.org)	Provides information, publications, and resources on staffing and talent management.
O*Net Center (online.onetcenter.org)	A government-provided source of occupational information useful for job analysis and labor market information.
Recruiting.org	Provides resources and information on recruiting and Internet recruiting.
Recruitingroundtable.com	Provides information, best practices, tools, metrics, and networking for recruiting executives.
Society for Human Resource Management (www.shrm.org)	Provides articles and other resources on staffing, including *Staffing Management* magazine.
Staffing.org	Has information and resources about staffing processes, practices, tools, and metrics.
Workforce Management (workforce.com)	Contains articles and resources on staffing and legal issues pertaining to staffing.
WorldatWork (worldatwork.org)	A not-for-profit professional association focusing on attracting, motivating, and retaining employees.

Summary

A firm's talent philosophy and business strategy are the basis for the HR strategy that guides its staffing strategy. Its talent philosophy reflects how it thinks about its employees. Its business strategies are created to leverage their resources and capabilities in ways that result in superior value creation compared to their competitors. Its competitive advantage depends on its ability to leverage the resources and capabilities that derive from the talent it is able to hire and retain. How it positions itself to compete in the marketplace determines the competitive advantage it needs to create and the staffing strategies it needs to pursue to acquire and retain the appropriate talent. A company's choice and execution of its staffing strategy influences the number and types of people it hires, and thus its ability to maintain a competitive advantage and execute its business strategy.

Endnotes

[1] See Phillips, J.M. & Gully, S.M. *Strategic Staffing*, 2009. Upper Saddle River, NJ: Prentice Hall.

[2] Michael V. Copeland, "My Golden Rule," *Business 2.0*, December 1, 2005, available online at: http://money.cnn.com/magazines/business2/business2_archive/2005/12/01/8364598/index.htm. Accessed February 15, 2009.

[3] Center for Advanced Human Resource Studies, "Time, Inc.," *hrSPECTRUM*, March-April 2004, p. 4. Available online at: http://www.ilr.cornell.edu/depts/cahrs/downloads/PDFs/hrSpectrum/HRSpec04-04.pdf. Accessed October 27, 2008.

[4] Porter, M.E., *Competitive Advantage: Creating and Sustaining Superior Performance*, 1985, New York: Free Press.

[5] Wright, P., McMahan, G., & McWilliams, A., "Human Resources and Sustained Competitive Advantage: A Resource-based Perspective," *International Journal of Human Resource Management*, 1994, 5, 301-26.

[6] Taylor, M.S. & Collins, C.J., "Organizational Recruitment: Enhancing the Intersection of Research and Practice," In G.L. Cooper & E.A. Locke, *Industrial and Organizational Psychology: What We Know About Theory & Practice*, 2000, Blackwells Oxford, UK: Blackwell Business, pp. 304-30.

[7] Barney, J., "Firm Resources and Sustained Competitive Advantage," *Journal of Management*, 1991, 17, 99-120.

[8] Grant, R., "The Resource-based Theory of Competitive Advantage: Implications for Strategy Formation," *California Management Review*, 1991, 33, 114-35.

[9] Barney, J., 1991; Barney, J. & Wright, P.M., "On Becoming a Strategic Partner: The Role of Human Resources in Gaining Competitive Advantage," *Human Resource Management*, Spring 1998, 31-46.

[10] Taylor, M.S. & Collins, C.J., 2000; Phillips, J.M., "Effects of realistic job previews on multiple organizational outcomes: A meta-analysis," *Academy of Management Journal*, 1998, 41, 673-690.

[11] Grant, L., "Happy Workers, High Returns," *Fortune*, January 12, 1998, 81-95.

[12] Taylor, M.S. & Collins, C.J., 2000.

[13] Ibid.

[14] Barney, J., 1991.

[15] Taylor, M.S. & Collins, C.J., 2000.

[16] Barney, J. & Wright, P.M., Spring 1998.

[17] Becker, B.E., Huselid, M.A., & Ulrich, D., *The HR Scorecard: Linking People, Strategy, and Performance*, 2001, Boston, MA: Harvard Business School Press.

[18] Pfeffer, J. *The Human Equation: Building Profits by Putting People First*, 1998, Boston: Harvard Business School Press.

[19] Grant, R. *Contemporary Strategy Analysis: Concepts, Techniques, Applications* (4th edition), 2002, Malden, MA: Blackwell Publishers, p. 13.

[20] Olian, J.D. & Rynes, S.L., "Organizational Staffing: Integrating Practice with Strategy," *Industrial Relations*, 23(2), Spring 1984, pp. 170-183.

[21] Treacy, M. and Wiersma, F. *The Discipline of Market Leaders*, 1997, Massachusetts: Perseus Books.

[22] Stanley Holmes and Wendy Zellner, "The Costco Way," *BusinessWeek Online*, April 12, 2004, http://www.businessweek.com/magazine/content/04_15/b3878084_mz021.htm.

[23] Porter, M.E., *Competitive Advantage*, 1985, New York: Free Press.

[24] Porter, M.E., 1985; Porter, M.E., 1998.

[25] Beatty, R.W. and Schneier, C.E., "New HR Roles to Impact Organizational Performance: From 'Partners' to 'Players,' " *Human Resource Management*, 1997, 36, 29-37; Deloitte & Touche, LLP, "Creating Shareholder Value Through People: The Human Capital ROI Study," 2002, New York: Deloitte & Touche, LLP; and Treacy, M. & Wiersema, F., "Customer Intimacy and Other Value Disciplines." *Harvard Business Review*, 1993, 71, 84-94.

[26] Ibid.

[27] Schuler, R. & Jackson, S., "Linking Competitive Strategies and Human Resource Management Practices," *Academy of Management Executive*, 1987, 1(3), pp. 207-219.

[28] Olian, J. & Rynes, S.L., 1984.

[29] Kiger, P.J., "Why Customer Satisfaction Starts With HR," *Workforce*, May 2002, 26-32.

[30] Beatty, R.W. and Schneier, C.E., 1997; Deloitte & Touche, LLP, 2002; and Treacy, M. & Wiersema, F., 1993.

[31] Excerpted from Johnson & Johnson, "Our Company," June 15, 2006, http://www.jnj.com/our_company/our_credo/index.htm;jsessionid=IQNLLJCS4XRLSCQPCB3SU0A. Accessed February 15, 2009.

[32] E.E. Hubbard, "Diversity Leadership By The Numbers: Implementing Diversity Management Strategies for Measurable Return on Investment (ROI) Performance," *News Brief of the MultiCultural Development Center*, May 25, 2006, available online at: http://view.exacttarget.com/?ffcb10-fe8e1277776d047f72-fdf017777d61057b76127273-ff2d17767060. Accessed February 15, 2009.

[33] Ibid.

[34] Mintz Levin, "Embracing Diversity," http://www.mintz.com/about/diversity/default.cfm. Accessed October 25, 2008.

[35] Dyer, L. & Holder, J., "A Strategic Perspective of Human Resource Management," In L. Dyer (ed.), *Human Resource Management: Evolving Roles and Responsibilities*, 1988, pp. 1-35. Washington, DC: American Society for Personnel Administration/Bureau of National Affairs.

36 The Ayers Group, "J&J Chairman Weldon Opens Ayers' Leadership Series," *The Ayers Report*, 2004, p. 2. Available online at: http://ayers.com/Summer_2004.pdf. Accessed June 6, 2006.
37 Sager, I., "Lou Takes the Gloves Off," *BusinessWeek*, November 18, 2002, 64-70.
38 Chambers, E.G., Foulon, M., Handfield-Jones, H., Hankin, S.M., & Michaels, E.G. III, "The War for Talent," *The McKinsey Quarterly*, 1998, 3, 44-57.
39 Baird, L. & Meshoulam, I., "Managing Two Fits of Strategic Human Resource Management," *Academy of Management Review*, 1988, 13, pp. 116-28; Lepak, D.P., Liao, H., Chung, Y., & Harden, E., "A Conceptual Review of Human Resource Management Systems in Strategic Human Resource Management Research," In J. Martocchio (ed.), *Research in Personnel and Human Resources Management*, 2006, Vol. 25, Stamford, CT: JAI Press; Huang, T.C., "The Effects of Linkage Between Business and Human Resource Management Strategies," *Personnel Review*, 2001, 30, 132-51.
40 Gupta, A.K. & Govindarajan, V., "Business Unit Strategy, Managerial Characteristics, and Business Unit Effectiveness at Strategy Implementation," *Academy of Management Journal*, 1984, 27, 25-41; Lundberg, C., "The Dynamic Organizational Contexts of Executive Succession: Considerations and Challenges," *Human Resource Management*, 1986, 25, 287-303.
41 Butler, J.E., Ferris, G.R., & Napier, N.K., *Strategy and Human Resources Management*, 1991, Cincinnati: South-Western.
42 Olian, J. & Rynes, S.L., "Organizational Staffing: Integrating Practice with Strategy," *Industrial Relations*, 1984, 23, 170-183.
43 "Career Opportunities," 3M Worldwide, available online at: http://cms.3m.com/cms/CA/en/1-30/criRrFN/view.jhtml. Accessed July 12, 2008.
44 Available online at: http://www.rmbh.co.za/citizenship.htm.
45 "McDonald's People Vision," McDonald's Corporation, available online at: http://www.rmhc.org/corp/values/ppromise/people_vision.html. Accessed July 10, 2008.
46 Ibid.
47 "McDonald's Commitment to Our Employees," McDonald's Corporation, available online at: http://www.rmhc.org/corp/values/ppromise/our_commitment.html. Accessed July 10, 2008.
48 Available online at: http://www.metso.com/reports/personnel/henkilosto_1_2.html. Accessed February 14, 2009.
49 Houseman, S.N., *Flexible Staffing Arrangements: A Report on Temporary Help, On-Call, Direct-Hire Temporary, Leased, Contract Company, and Independent Contractor Employment in the United States*, A publication of the W.E. UpJohn Institute for Employment Research. August 1999.
50 Caudron, S., "Calculating the Cost of Contingent Workers," *Personnel Journal*, November 1994, 73(11), pp. 48a-48c.
51 "Hamburger University—McDonald's Center of Training Excellence," available online at: http://www.mcdonalds.com/corp/career/hamburger_university.html. Accessed February 13, 2009.
52 Ibid.

[53] Solomon, C.M. (1998), "Stellar recruiting for a tight labor market," *Workforce*, August, 77, 66-71.
[54] Miner, A. "Idiosyncratic jobs in formal organizations," *Administrative Science Quarterly*, 1987, 32, 327-51.
[55] Krell, E. (2002). "Recruiting Outlook: Creative HR for 2003," *Workforce*, December, 81, 40-5.
[56] Soper, N.A. (2001). *Recruitment & retention lessons from industry and high tech organizations: Winning the war for scientists and engineers.* Air Force Research Laboratory, Space Vehicles Directorate, Kirtland Air Force Base. Available online at: http://www.afpc.randolph.af.mil/cp/secp/Documents/Summary%20of%20 Industry%20Visits.doc. Accessed July 22, 2008.
[57] Colvin, G., "How to Get Your Head Around Measuring Minds," *Fortune*, December 20, 1999, p. 334-335.
[58] Kelley, R. & Caplan, J., "How Bell Labs Create Star Performers," *Harvard Business Review*, July-August 1993, 128-139.
[59] Hunter, J.E., Schmidt, F.L., & Judiesch, M.K., "Individual Differences in Output Variability as a Function of Job Complexity," *Journal of Applied Psychology*, 1990, 75, 28-42.
[60] Phillips, J.M., 1998.
[61] Boudreau, J.W., "Utility Analysis for Decisions in Human Resource Management," In M.D. Dunnette and L.M. Hough (eds.), *Handbook of Industrial and Organizational Psychology*, vol. 2, 1991, Palo Alto, CA: Consulting Psychologists Press, pp. 601-17.
[62] Weber, G., "Preserving the Starbucks' Counter Culture," *Workforce Management*, February 2005, pp. 28-34.
[63] Martinez, M.N., "Recruiting Here and There," *HR Magazine*, September 2002, 47, 95-100.
[64] Lado, A.A. & Wilson, M.C., "Human Resource Systems and Sustained Competitive Advantage: A Competency-Based Perspective," *Academy of Management Review*, 1994, 19(4), pp. 699-727.
[65] Boxall, P., "The Strategic Human Resource Management Debate and the Resource-based View of the Firm," *Human Resource Management Journal*, 1996, 6, 59-75.
[66] Harris, B.R., Huselid, M.A., & Becker, B.E., "Strategic Human Resource Management at Praxair," *Human Resource Management*, 1999, 38, 315-20.
[67] Rynes, S.L. & Barber, A.E. (1990), "Applicant attraction strategies: An organizational perspective," *Academy of Management Review*, 15, 286-310.

Index

3M 4, 13, 28, 29

A
Accountemps 32
active learners 14
Allied Signal 27
Apple Computer 4, 12

B
Ballmer, Steve 1
Barney, Jay 4
Bell Labs 41
Bessey, Kerry 1
Bossidy, Larry 27
business priorities 43
business strategy/strategies 2, 9, 10, 11, 15, 17, 19, 27, 28, 33, 39, 40, 52, 55, 57
    cost leadership strategy 11-12, 14, 15, 18
    differentiation strategy 11, 12-13, 17
    execution 1, 27
    influences 28
    specialization strategy 11, 14-15
    types of 10-16

C
candidate pool 43
career development 33
Carter's 12
compensation 7, 19, 27
competency/competencies 3, 16, 28, 42, 44, 48, 52
competitive advantage 1, 2, 3, 4, 5, 6, 7, 9, 10, 12, 13, 14, 15, 27, 40, 47, 48, 49, 57
    requirements 5
    sources 10
competitive environment 9, 16
competitive success 27
Container Store, The 39
contingent workers 31, 32
Corning 23
Costco 5, 10
cost-per-hire 51
culture of inclusion 22
culture(s) 6, 16, 22
    innovative culture 13
    organizational 35

customer demographics 11
customer intimacy 14
customer loyalty 14
customer relationships 54
customer services 9
    strategy 33

D
Dell Computers 12, 40, 41
deregulation 11, 15
diversity 21, 22, 28, 37
    goals 37
    organizational 35

E
economic downturns 48
EDS 37
emotional resilience 14
employee development 48
employee motivation 35
employee productivity 10
employee tenure 54
employment assessment 33
entrepreneurial environment 13
equal opportunity 20
Ernst & Young 5
ethical behavior 23
ethical guidelines 24
ethical issues 23, 24
ethical principles 20
ethical standards 23
ethical values 24
external hires 17, 35

F
fairness 23
Federal Express 12, 32, 40
flexible workers 31, 32
Fortune 1

G
Genentech 23
General Electric 9
Georgia-Pacific 32
Gerstner, Lou 27
global marketplace 22

Google 4, 5
growth strategy 15-16, 29

H
Hamburger University 34
Hewitt Associates 45
hiring 9, 33, 47, 54
    discrimination 37
    goals 51
    guidelines 44
    internal 35
    managers 36, 44, 53, 54
    process 38
honesty 23
human capital 22
    human capital advantage 47
human process advantage 47
human resources (HR)
    activities 7, 30
    expenditures 42
    function 19, 27, 29
        functional area 29
    management 4, 19
        functions 8
        policies and practices 9
        system 8
    policies 30
    practices 3, 16
    strategic HR management 19
    strategy/strategies 2, 18, 19, 26, 27, 29, 30, 57
    systems 27
Hyundai 4

I
IBM 9, 27
idiosyncratic jobs 38
ING Direct 12
inimitability 6
innovation 7, 17, 21, 28, 47
innovative organizations 13
integrity 23
Intel 17
intellectual capital 1
internal job candidates 34
internal promotions 35
internal training 35
investor preferences 15

J
job analysis 28, 36
job description 54
job security 31
job-oriented philosophy 39
job-oriented staffing 38
Johnson & Johnson 13, 20, 24, 38
judgment 7

K
Kelly Services 32
Kroc, Ray 34

L
labor 16, 22
    costs 5, 27, 47
    demand 48
    market(s) 6, 38, 44
    pool 48
    supply 36
layoffs 32
leadership 30
    future leaders 41
    future leadership 21
    positions 33
Lexus 1, 12
life cycle 17-18
    decline 18
    growth 17
    introduction 17
    maturity 18
low-cost strategy 23, 27

M
managing talent 23
Manpower 32
market compensation rates 17
market segment 14
market share 17
market wages 34
McDonald's 29, 30, 34
McDonnell Douglas 32
Mercedes 12
mergers and acquisitions 15, 16
metrics 45
Metso 29, 30
Microsoft 1, 4
Mintz Levin 22
motivations 3

N
Nike 13
Nokia 21

O
operational efficiencies 16
organizational capability 1
organizational flexibility 13
organizational performance 23

P
pay-for-performance system 13
People 1
People Promise 29
People Vision 29
performance 5, 35
    management 19
        functions 27
Pfizer 4, 23

Porter, Michael 11
Praxair 48
PricewaterhouseCoopers Saratoga 2005/2006 Human Capital Index Report 41
Procter & Gamble 1, 9
product development 13
product innovation 12, 23
product market maturity 11
productivity 5, 41

R

recruiting 37, 43
    initiative 6
    networks 6
    source 37
    sources 55
recruitment 7, 41
    goals 51
    sources 23
Red Lobster 14
resource-based view 3, 4
resources 9
retaining 47
retention 5, 27, 35, 41, 42, 54
RMB Holdings 29
Rolex 12

S

Sam's Club 10
SAS 54
scarce talent 38
Seiko 14
selection 7
    methods 23
South Africa 29
Southern, Sheri 44
Southwest Airlines 12
specialization 18
Sports Illustrated 1
staffing
    activities 5, 41
    centralized staffing function 43
    conduct 24
    costs 51
    decentralized staffing 43
        function 44
    decisions 36
    effort(s) 16, 52, 53, 55
    function 7, 8, 44
    goal(s) 12, 23, 51, 52, 53, 54, 55
        outcome goals 51, 52
    influences 3
    initiative 6
    investment(s) 5, 17, 51
    issues 39
    metrics 44
    needs 2
    nontraditional 32
    philosophy 24, 43
    pipeline 38
    practices 28, 37, 47
    proactive 37
    process 43
    process goals 51, 52
    professionals 44
    resources 56
    specialists 24
    standards and ethical guidelines, sources for 25
    strategy/strategies 2, 15, 18, 21, 22, 26, 29, 32, 39, 42, 52, 57
        elements of 31
    system 42, 55
stakeholders 19
Starbucks 4, 14, 15, 44
strategic capability 4
strategic challenge 27
strategic change 16
strategic choice 21, 38, 54
strategic performance 51
strategic staffing 52
    goals 53
    practices 6
    process 51
strategy choice 27
strategy execution 27
strategy implementation 16
substitutability 7
succession planning 33
sustainable competitive advantage 5, 7

T

talent(s) 1, 2, 3, 5, 6, 7, 12, 15, 16, 17, 33, 37, 47, 52, 53
    acquisition 27, 48
    external talent focus 18, 33, 34, 35
    internal 18, 35
        focus 33, 35
        leadership talent 33
    management 20
    mixes 53
    needs 54
    philosophy/philosophies 16, 18, 19, 20, 21, 22, 23, 26, 28, 31, 33, 38, 39, 57
        asset-based talent philosophy 23
    pool 27, 55
        internal 17, 48
    reserves 48
    sources 6
    strategy 19, 39
    talent 16
teamwork 12
technology/technologies 7, 36, 54
temporary workers 32
Time, Inc. 1
training 27, 30, 33
    costs 21, 41
    system 7
Treacy, Michael 9
turnover 5, 21, 23, 27, 34, 53, 54

U
unintended strategies 17
UPS 32

V
values 52
    creation 5

W
Wal-Mart 11, 12
Whirlpool 23
Wiersma, Fred 9
workforce 10
    adaptability 54
    attributes 5

Acknowledgments

We would like to thank our sons, Ryan and Tyler, for their support and patience while we wrote this book. We would also like to thank Pearson for allowing us to adapt some of the material from our book, *Strategic Staffing*, for use in this series. We also thank the reviewers—especially Laura Ostroff, director of Total Rewards and HRIS, Bon Secours Health System, Inc.—and the SHRM staff for this opportunity and for their suggestions and insights. If you have feedback about this book or if you would like to contact us for any reason, please e-mail us at phillipsgully@gmail.com.

About the Authors

Jean M. Phillips, Ph.D., is an associate professor of human resource management at the School of Management and Labor Relations, Rutgers University. Dr. Phillips is a current or former member of several editorial boards including *Personnel Psychology, Journal of Applied Psychology,* and *Journal of Management.* She received the 2004 Cummings Scholar Award from the Organizational Behavior Division of the Academy of Management and was among the top five percent of published authors in two of the top human resource management journals during the 1990s. She is also the co-author of the college textbooks *Managing Now!* (2007) and *Strategic Staffing* (2008) and consults in the areas of recruiting and staffing, linking employee surveys to organizational outcomes, and team effectiveness. She can be reached at phillipsgully@gmail.com

Stanley M. Gully, Ph.D., is an associate professor of human resource management at the School of Management and Labor Relations, Rutgers University. He is a current or former member of the editorial boards of *Academy of Management Journal, Journal of Applied Psychology, Journal of Organizational Behavior,* and *Journal of Management.* He received multiple awards for his teaching, research, and service, including a research award from the American Society for Training & Development. His paper on general self-efficacy is in the top 10 most read papers in *Organizational Research Methods* and his meta-analysis on cohesion is in the top three most cited papers in Small Group Research. He is the co-author of *Strategic Staffing* (2008) and consults in the areas of recruiting and staffing, employee engagement, team effectiveness, and organizational learning interventions. He can be reached at phillipsgully@gmail.com

Additional SHRM-Published Books

The Cultural Fit Factor: Creating an Employment Brand that Attracts, Retains, and Repels the Right Employees
By Lizz Pellet

The Employer's Immigration Compliance Desk Reference
By Gregory H. Siskind

Employment Termination Source Book
By Wendy Bliss and Gene Thornton

The Essential Guide to Workplace Investigations: How to Handle Employee Complaints & Problems
By Lisa Guerin

Hiring Source Book
By Catherine D. Fyock

Hiring Success: The Art and Science of Staffing Assessment and Employee Selection
By Steven Hunt

Human Resource Essentials: Your Guide to Starting and Running the HR Function
By Lin Grensing-Pophal

Leading With Your Heart: Diversity and Ganas for Inspired Inclusion
By Cari M. Dominguez and Jude Sotherlund

Outsourcing Human Resources Functions: How, Why, When, and When Not to Contract for HR Services, 2d ed.
By Mary F. Cook and Scott B. Gildner

Smart Policies for Workplace Technologies: E-mail, Blogs, Cell Phones and More
By Lisa Guerin

Stop Bullying at Work: Strategies and Tools for HR and Legal Professionals
By Teresa A. Daniel

Strategic Staffing: A Comprehensive System for Effective Workforce Planning, 2nd ed.
By Thomas P. Bechet

For these and other SHRM-published books, please visit www.shrm.org/publications/books/pages/default.aspx.